EDI

THE C

New Tov
Comprisi
cobbled s.   gardens, the
New Town is urban-planning perfection.

Melville Monument
Architect William Burn based this 1821 tribute
to Viscount Melville, aka 'The Uncrowned King
of Scotland', on Trajan's Column in Rome. At
41m tall, it fairly lords it over the New Town.
St Andrew Square

Royal Scottish Academy
Reopened in 2003, the RSA hosts world-class
exhibitions. The next-door Scottish National
Gallery (T 624 6200) displays art from the
Renaissance era to the late 19th century.
The Mound, T 225 6671

Princes Street Gardens
Avoid the bustle and crush of shoppers along
the main drag of Princes Street with a detour
through this pretty, peaceful park.

Scott Monument
George Meikle Kemp's 61m-high monument
in honour of Sir Walter Scott was unveiled in
1846. Some see it as an example of neo-Gothic
splendour, others as an ancient space rocket.
East Princes Street Gardens

The Balmoral
Opened in 1902 as the North British Hotel,
this behemoth links the architecture of the
Old Town with the neoclassicism of the New.
See p016

Calton Hill
Climb up this magnificent incline to marvel
at the breathtaking panorama and the tower
celebrating Nelson's 1805 Trafalgar victory.
See p013

INTRODUCTION
THE CHANGING FACE OF THE URBAN SCENE

If looks alone were the measure of a city, then the Scottish capital would rank among the finest in the world. The dizzyingly romantic cobblestoned streets and medieval architecture of the Old Town are astonishingly intact and the Georgian splendour of the New Town's broad avenues and sweeping terraces is enough to give the first-time visitor goosebumps. But don't think that this is a city trading solely on its beauty – if you get to know it, you will discover it has a sharp, witty personality to match. Edinburgh is a centre for the arts. It has an impressive range of galleries and theatres, it boasts a respected university and a slew of bookish cafés. However, just because the city is well read, that doesn't mean it goes to bed early. The capital's pubs are renowned for their relaxed licensing hours and its bars know how to mix a decent cocktail or two.

Devolution in 1999 brought a new-found confidence, and the city has been moving forward ever since – perfectly content with its status quo to overwhelmingly vote 'No' in the 2014 referendum for Scottish independence. Huge sums have been spent sprucing up the old port of Leith, renovating national galleries and bringing trams to the centre. As far as new developments go, transport still gets top billing. A fast airport link, which was completed in 2014, the refurbished Waverley Station and, due in 2017, the Queensferry Crossing, will ensure that whichever route you take to Edinburgh, first impressions will be of its bold 21st-century achievements.

ESSENTIAL INFO
FACTS, FIGURES AND USEFUL ADDRESSES

TOURIST OFFICE
Edinburgh Information Centre
3 Princes Street
T 0845 225 5121
www.visitscotland.com

TRANSPORT
Airport transfer to city centre
Trams depart regularly from 6.15am until
10.45pm. The journey takes 35 minutes
www.edinburghtrams.com
Bus
Lothian Buses
T 555 6363
Car hire
Hertz
10 Picardy Place
T 0843 309 3026
Taxi
City Cabs
T 228 1211
There are plenty of taxi ranks and black
cabs can be safely hailed on the street
Travel Card
The seven-day Ridacard grants unlimited
travel on bus services and trams for £18

EMERGENCY SERVICES
Emergencies
T 999
Late-night pharmacy
Boots
46-48 Shandwick Place
T 225 6757
Open until 8pm, Monday to Friday;
6pm on Saturdays; 5pm on Sundays

CONSULATES
US Consulate General
3 Regent Terrace
T 556 8315
edinburgh.usconsulate.gov

POSTAL SERVICES
Post office
5-6 Waverley Mall Shopping Centre
T 524 6901
Shipping
UPS
30 South Gyle Crescent

BOOKS
Exit Music by Ian Rankin (Orion)
**Of Its Time and Of Its Place: The Work
of Richard Murphy Architects**
by Richard MacCormac (Black Dog)
The Prime of Miss Jean Brodie
by Muriel Spark (Penguin Classics)

WEBSITES
Architecture
www.edinburgharchitecture.co.uk
Art
www.nationalgalleries.org
Newspaper
www.scotsman.com

EVENTS
Edinburgh Festival Fringe
www.edfringe.com
Edinburgh International Book Festival
www.edbookfest.co.uk

COST OF LIVING
**Taxi from Edinburgh Airport
to city centre**
£20
Cappuccino
£2.60
Packet of cigarettes
£10
Daily newspaper
£1
Bottle of champagne
£35

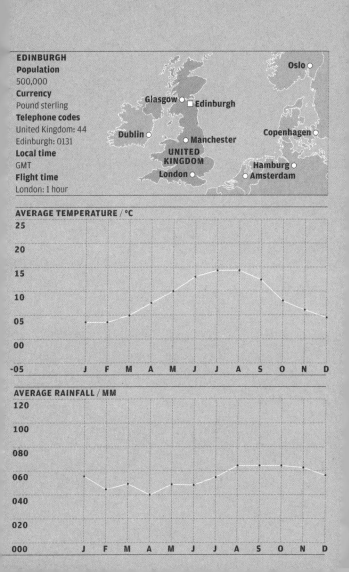

EDINBURGH
Population
500,000
Currency
Pound sterling
Telephone codes
United Kingdom: 44
Edinburgh: 0131
Local time
GMT
Flight time
London: 1 hour

AVERAGE TEMPERATURE / °C

	J	F	M	A	M	J	J	A	S	O	N	D
25												
20												
15												
10												
05												
00												
-05												

AVERAGE RAINFALL / MM

	J	F	M	A	M	J	J	A	S	O	N	D
120												
100												
080												
060												
040												
020												
000												

NEIGHBOURHOODS
THE AREAS YOU NEED TO KNOW AND WHY

To help you navigate the city, we've chosen the most interesting districts (see below and the map inside the back cover) and colour-coded our featured venues, according to their location; those venues that are outside these areas are not coloured.

LEITH
Irvine Welsh's 1993 novel *Trainspotting* put the city's downtrodden port on the map. Two decades on and, although some rough edges remain, Leith is transformed. Galleries, waterfront bars and cafés are blossoming. At the heart of the district's regeneration is food. Alongside a clutch of gastropubs, the neighbourhood also lays claim to a pair of Michelin-starred restaurants: The Kitchin (see p047) and Martin Wishart (see p058).

SOUTHSIDE/NEWINGTON
Largely residential, this is the city's least characterful corner. But it is home to the Festival Theatre (13-29 Nicholson Street, T 529 6000) and, during the Festival, the Pleasance Theatre (60 Pleasance, T 650 4199). Other draws are music venue The Queen's Hall (85-89 Clerk Street, T 668 2019), the Royal Commonwealth Pool (see p078), several university buildings and Foster + Partners' Quartermile.

NEW TOWN
This UNESCO World Heritage site was designed in 1767 by a young Edinburgh-born architect named James Craig. The grand Georgian terraces and their elegant neoclassical details have been exquisitely maintained. Originally intended as an area purely for housing, the New Town now offers boutique hotels, like The Howard (see p016), and an impressive array of independent stores (see p090).

OLD TOWN
The city's core of medieval architecture and cobbled wynds dates back to the 12th century. Another UNESCO World Heritage site, it is centred around the Royal Mile, which leads to the domineering Edinburgh Castle (see p010). To the south lies the Continental-style boulevard Grassmarket, lined with lively cafés and pubs. The area teems with ghost tours and tat shops, but it's near impossible not to be impressed by all the magnificent history on show.

WEST END/TOLLCROSS/BRUNTSFIELD
It may not be as picturesque as the Old or New Towns, but the West End does host several key arts venues, including Usher Hall (Lothian Road, T 228 1155). To the south-west, Tollcross has a somewhat seamy side to it, but emerging from this scruffy charm is Bruntsfield. Formerly a quarantine zone for plague victims, it's now a buzzy hub of boutiques, delis and handsome Victorian tenement buildings.

CANONGATE
Essentially the lower part of the Royal Mile, this district brims with history and tourist attractions, including the Dynamic Earth exhibition (112-116 Holyrood Gait, T 550 7801), by Hopkins Architects, and John Knox House (see p081). The arrival of the bold, frenetic Scottish Parliament (see p076), opposite the Holyrood Palace (T 556 5100), has transformed Canongate into a must-visit neighbourhood.

LANDMARKS

THE SHAPE OF THE CITY SKYLINE

Climb up any of Edinburgh's reputed 'Seven Hills', look down at the capital below and you'll see that the city is quite a staggering landmark in itself. The sheer lack of 20th-century development in the centre means that, on a clear day, as you survey the Gothic spires and blackened turrets towards the dramatic coastline that edges the Firth of Forth estuary, it really is a sight to behold.

In terms of highlights, no one building shouts 'landmark' louder than Edinburgh Castle (overleaf). Built on a craggy escarpment as a medieval stronghold, often targeted by the English, it dominates the skyline and was the seat of Scottish royalty. It is the point from which the rest of Edinburgh has grown, and is a helpful navigational tool. A pinnacle of the old town, it acts as a striking contrast to the surrounding 18th- and 19th-century architecture.

This 'newer' development encompasses the poignant and much-loved National Monument on Calton Hill (see p013), while more flamboyant buildings such as McEwan Hall (see p012), which was completed in 1897, show the extravagance that was lavished on the city during the Victorian era. Further evidence of this can be found if you make the short drive out to the Forth Rail Bridge (see p014). A masterpiece of engineering that's more than 125 years old, this magnificent steel structure is as admired by locals as it is by visitors, and was granted UNESCO World Heritage status in 2015. *For full addresses, see Resources.*

Edinburgh Castle

Looming over the capital from its perch on Castle Rock, this sprawling, multi-levelled ensemble of historical buildings enclosed within sheer battlement walls certainly makes its forbidding presence felt. The oldest part dates from 1130, and it housed the Scottish royal family until 1603, when James VI became James I of England. The highlights of its various museum displays include the Honours (crown jewels), which were first used together at the coronation of the nine-month-old Mary, Queen of Scots in 1543; and the Stone of Destiny, which was finally returned in 1996, some 700 years after Edward I took it from Scone, near Perth, and had it built into his throne at Westminster Abbey. Sure, it's a tourist magnet, but its majesty surpasses most. *Castle Hill, T 225 9846, www.edinburghcastle.gov.uk*

McEwan Hall

Edinburgh's students have long chuckled at the irony of graduating in a building bearing the same name as the beer that often distracted them from studying for their degrees. Irony aside, the university was fortunate that a substantial donation from prosperous Scottish brewery owner William McEwan financed the construction of this neoclassical amphitheatre. Finished in 1897, it was the most flamboyant design of architect Sir Robert Rowand Anderson, who was also responsible for the Scottish National Portrait Gallery (see p034). If you like the extravagance of the exterior (the stonework was extensively restored in 2015), William M Palin's murals ensure the interior is equally impressive. Added in 2017, a rounded glass entrance pavilion by LDN now emboldens Bristo Square.
Bristo Square

National Monument

The summit of Calton Hill, with its grassy slopes and panoramic views, is probably one of the first places that a local will take you. Yet despite its popularity and central location, the peak, reached via a steep staircase climbing up the hill from Waterloo Place, is a delightfully peaceful spot to spend half an hour or so. Next to the Nelson Monument, you'll see this bizarre acropolis-style folly, designed by English architect Charles Robert Cockerell and Scotsman William Playfair. Modelled on the Parthenon in Athens and dedicated to those who perished in the Napoleonic Wars, its construction began in 1824 but it was never fully completed. At the time, this was seen as a national scandal. Today, however, it only adds to the lyrical feel of this characterful patch of Edinburgh.
Calton Hill

Forth Rail Bridge

It is perhaps indicative of Edinburgh's good fortune that although it was hardly touched by the Industrial Revolution (the city remained essentially professional), it still benefited from the most expensive, most beautiful feat of Victorian British engineering. The Forth Rail Bridge was designed by Sir Benjamin Baker and Sir John Fowler and completed in 1890; the cantilevered steel structure rises imperiously from the Firth of Forth, and stretches 2.5km across the estuary to Fife. Despite the popular myth that repainting the bridge is an endless task, the job was completed, ahead of schedule, in 2011. Trainspotting in this town may have taken on new meaning thanks to Irvine Welsh, but as far as the hobby goes, there is no better place to do it than here.
Queensferry

HOTELS

WHERE TO STAY AND WHICH ROOMS TO BOOK

For such a small city, Edinburgh attracts a huge number of visitors. At Hogmanay and during the Festival, there's no room at the inn, but booking well ahead is advisable over the rest of the summer as well. The grand Georgian residences in the New Town make perfect boutique hotels, but with only a handful of rooms in each, they fill up quickly. For this kind of intimate accommodation, The Howard (34 Great King Street, T 557 3500) and the Nira Caledonia (6-10 Gloucester Place, T 225 2720) are both good options. Or stay at a self-catering property, such as the chic, albeit out-of-the-way Pavilion (see p021). If you crave five-star facilities and a central location, two luxuriously reworked railway hotels stand sentinel at either end of Princes Street: Rocco Forte's The Balmoral (No 1, T 556 2414) and The Caledonian (see p061); or book the stylish Principal (19-21 George Street, T 225 1251), situated inside a string of listed townhouses. At the other end of the spectrum, the first UK property from savvy German chain Motel One (18-21 Market Street, T 220 0730) opened in the capital in 2012, and a second site followed in 2014 (10-15 Princes Street, T 550 9220).

For more contemporary environs, The Glasshouse (2 Greenside Place, T 525 8200), which promises large rooms and an abundance of outdoor space, provides a modern take on the traditional Scottish interior, whereas Tigerlily (see p019) is best for party animals. *For full addresses and room rates, see Resources.*

The Witchery

If you are looking for eccentricity, opt for one of the 10 theatrical suites located at the top of a winding stone staircase above James Thomson's celebrated restaurant of the same name, and across the street in a second historic building. This is Gothic glamour at its most extreme, each room boasting antiques and curiosities, roll-top baths for two people and complimentary champagne; many also have four-posters draped in velvet. Forget the wi-fi, plasma screens and power showers; The Witchery is all about romance. Think Versace does Victoriana and you will be some of the way to envisaging the lust den that is the Old Rectory. Alternatively, book the Heriot Suite for its chapel bathroom (above) and the panoramic views across the Old Town. *Castlehill, The Royal Mile, T 225 5613, www.thewitchery.com*

G&V Royal Mile

Formerly the Hotel Missoni, this modern pile was revamped in 2014 and reopened as the George & Victoria. A collection of Scottish designers set the tone: doormen don kilts with a contemporary edge by Howie Nicholsby, and staff wear hand-tailored uniforms by Judy R Clark, which combine Harris tweeds, lace and antique fabric. Alongside 127 rooms, there are nine suites each kitted out by a local maker, including artist Hatti Pattisson, who conceived the vivid floral textiles in the Garden Paradise Suite (above); and Glasgow firm Timorous Beasties, whose eponymous digs feature a surreal thistle-print wallpaper. The Epicurean bar on the ground floor is a swish place for a cocktail, and upstairs is Italian restaurant Cucina.
1 George IV Bridge, T 220 6666,
www.quorvuscollection.com

Tigerlily

This rock'n'roll hotel seemingly makes no attempt at self-restraint, much like its club, Lulu (T 225 5005), in the basement, or shimmering street-level bar (above), which has a bolshy, inventive cocktail list; the Tiger Never Dies combines Appleton and Wray & Nephew rums, pink grapefruit, cinnamon syrup, bitters and an absinthe rinse. But the 33 rooms are more than just a place to lay your head after a few too many and are, in fact, very chic. Reserve the glamorous, well-equipped Georgian Suite, which features a huge four-poster bed and a separate lounge area; or the moody Black Room, tucked away at the top of the building and fitted with a modern fireplace. There are also White Company bathroom products and in-room iPods.
125 George Street, T 225 5005,
www.tigerlilyedinburgh.co.uk

94DR

One of the best features of this 21st-century B&B is also the worst – its location. On a busy road in Southside, a 10-minute ride from the centre, what 94DR lacks in convenience it makes up for in the sense of calm you get from staying at arm's length from the hordes. Paul Lightfoot and John MacEwan have eschewed the usual swathes of ubiquitous tartan found in the city's guesthouses;

their elegant townhouse has real style. Flowers brighten its tiled entrance hall, cooked-to-order breakfasts are seasonal, there is an honesty bar, and attention to detail is such that showers have taps set to one side so that you don't get a wet arm when you switch them on. The Bowmore (pictured) is our room key of choice.
94 Dalkeith Road, T 662 9265,
www.94dr.com

The Pavilion at Lamb's House

Designed by architect Nicholas Groves-Raines, who lives with his wife Kristin Hannesdottir in the restored 17th-century Lamb's House next door, The Pavilion is a self-contained, three-storey new-build, styled as an 18th-century garden home. Groves-Raines' speciality is conservation, and it's evident in the fine detail at play here, from the ogee roof to the antique furnishings. The abode sleeps six people across three bedrooms, including a pretty twin with dove-grey walls, and another with a box bed encased in mustard-hued panelling. There's a freestanding tub in the bathroom, and a wood-burning fireplace, just begging to be cranked up, in the living quarters. This is an ideal base from which to explore the revitalised docks district.
11 Waters' Close, T 467 7777,
www.lambspavilion.com

Prestonfield
This 17th-century mansion was home to the Dick-Cunyngham family for 300 years. A hotel for five decades, it has hosted guests like Oliver Reed and Joan Collins. Many of the 23 rooms and suites, including the lavish Benjamin Franklin (pictured), are decked out with sleigh beds and indecent amounts of silk. For a decadent weekend, it's hard to beat. *Priestfield Road, T 225 7800*

24 HOURS

SEE THE BEST OF THE CITY IN JUST ONE DAY

If you take just one piece of advice when in Edinburgh, it should be to wear comfortable shoes. Although there is no shortage of taxis around for late nights and the inevitable cloudbursts, if you don't put in the legwork you'll miss out on what makes this capital so impressive. Shortcuts through its cobbled streets and hidden closes will reveal tucked-away galleries, unassuming eateries and small shops selling craft wares. Alternatively, you might fancy the promenade along the redeveloped docks at Leith (see p045), or the climb up Arthur's Seat or Calton Hill (see p032) to admire the view.

Edinburgh is wonderfully compact, and it's possible to fit in a far-reaching itinerary. Having said that, it would be near impossible to attempt everything we have suggested here, and you may have to pick and choose, whether you're of the sporting persuasion – one of the world's top climbing centres (see p027) and an 1897 pool (see p038) are architectural marvels – or prefer to immerse yourself in the resurgent art scene (see p064). Fortunately there are plenty of fine places to refuel as you plot your course. Kick off with coffee at Cairngorm (opposite) or eggs at Urban Angel (121 Hanover Street, T 225 6215), and stop for lunch at The Dogs (see p030), which serves hearty fare with a retro flavour. By night, strike out to Edinburgh Food Studio (see p039) before heading to the gin bar at Stac Polly (29-33 Dublin Street, T 556 2231) or the Whiski Rooms (see p040). *For full addresses, see Resources.*

09.00 Cairngorm Coffee

A champion of the city's third-wave coffee scene, Robi Lambie launched Cairngorm in 2014 through a cosy venue on Frederick Street (T 629 1420), and this branch was opened in 2016. Lambie worked with young architect Matt Smith and local firm Splintr on the bright, polished interiors, which feature high tables made from ashwood and brushed copper, and industrial-style pendant lights from London's Horsfall & Wright. The café collaborates with a bevy of speciality roasters, most of which are Scandinavian, like Good Life, Obadiah and La Cabra – the Sanremo Opera espresso machine was the very first of its kind in Scotland. The food is simple but tasty. Try a grilled sandwich that drips with melted cheese sourced from IJ Mellis (see p088). *1 Melville Place, T 629 1420, www.cairngormcoffee.com*

09.45 Ruffians

You may arrive here hirsute and unkempt, but by the time you have been primped and preened at this concept salon you will be every inch the metrosexual. The retro design belies its 21st-century ethos, one that celebrates the barber's ancient art by taking it to another level. The six-step Hot Shave consists of a pampering face scrub, a hot towel, a cut-throat shave, an iced towel, a facial moisturiser and a shoulder, arm and head massage, all using Ruffians' bespoke range of male grooming products. The interior, masterminded by Glasgow-based Graven Images, features dark indigo paintwork, vintage Japanese hairdressing chairs, subway tiles and a slick 'waiting room' with a row of iPads as an alternative to crumpled newspapers. *23 Queensferry Street, T 225 8962, www.ruffians.co.uk*

10.45 EICA

As the largest indoor climbing facility in the world, the Edinburgh International Climbing Arena (EICA) won a place in the record books for its hometown of Ratho, 20 minutes west of Edinburgh. The state-of-the-art venue is the creation of two local aficionados, Rab Anderson and Duncan McCallum, who teamed up with architect David Taylor to create a five-storey structure built into a 32.5m disused quarry. This engineering feat means the centre not only offers 3,000 sq m of artificial climbing, but it is the only indoor complex on the planet that boasts natural rock walls. There is also an aerial rope course, an adventure sports gym, a health club, cafés and a lecture theatre, plus various bouldering problems to solve. *South Platt Hill, Ratho, Newbridge, T 333 6333, www.eica-ratho.com*

12.00 Fruitmarket Gallery

There are no prizes for guessing that this contemporary art space occupies a former fruit and veg market, built in 1938. It was transformed into a gallery in 1974 and remodelled in 1993 by architects Richard Murphy, who introduced a 'floating' roof, allowing natural light to flood the first floor, and a central steel staircase, which can be elevated to make way for large installations. It has shown works by high-profile international artists, including Louise Bourgeois, Dieter Roth and Martin Creed (see p070), as well as Scots Lucy Skaer and Nathan Coley. Mexican talent Damián Ortega's 2016 show 'Stages of Time' (right) included a collection of clay sculptures, laid out on high tables as if unearthed in an archaeological dig. There is also an on-site bookshop and café.
45 Market Street, T 225 2383,
www.fruitmarket.co.uk

13.00 The Dogs

David Ramsden's shabby-chic gastropub, which occupies a first-floor Georgian apartment, is a perennial favourite with locals. The kitchen conjures up delicious modern Scottish food, like slow-cooked venison, smoked haddock fish cakes, and a haggis and Cumberland sausage hash in whisky sauce. Such unaffected dining is still hard to find in the city.
110 Hanover Street, T 220 1208

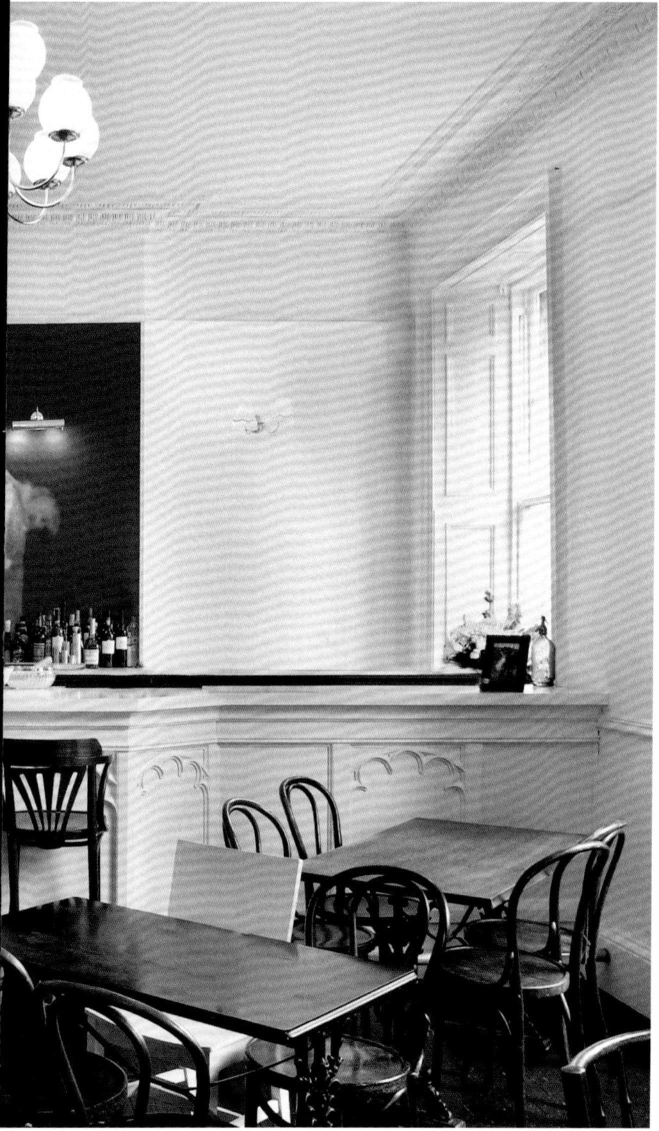

14.15 Collective

Established in 1984, the not-for-profit arts organisation Collective decamped from Cockburn Street to this historic site on Calton Hill (see p013) in 2013. The complex encompasses William Playfair's City Dome (pictured, right) and the city's former observatory (slated to open in 2017), both of which have been restored and fitted out to house exhibition space. There's a new subterranean gallery too, as well as a restaurant, a shop, and the open-air Milk kiosk (T 551 5775). Since its inception, Collective has supported a wide-reaching programme of art – from Laura Yuile's video works to Conor Kelly's sculptures and an installation by Marie-Michelle Deschamps – and an engaging series of satellite projects and events. *38 Calton Hill, T 556 1264, www.collectivegallery.net*

15.15 Scottish National Portrait Gallery

Reinvigorated in 2011 by Glasgow's Page\
Park firm after a three-year £17.6m refurb,
the SNPG is now closer to architect Sir
Robert Rowand Anderson's original 1889
designs than it was for much of the 20th
century. Visitors can access three floors
here and a further showcase of its portrait
and photography collections in new spaces
including the Contemporary Gallery. An
increase in natural light has been made
possible by the removal of partitions and
suspended ceilings, all the better to see
Alexander Nasmyth's painting of Robert
Burns, and Robert Adamson and David
Octavius Hill's 19th-century photograph
of a Newhaven fishwife. The magnificent
suite of exhibition rooms on the top floor
(Gallery Five, above) should not be missed.
1 Queen Street, T 624 6200,
www.nationalgalleries.org

16.30 Number Shop

This artist-run space was established by young sculptor Alistair Grant in 2014 to support early-career artists. The low-slung block (formerly an adult education centre for maths, hence the name), dressed up with strips of Mondrian-like colour, houses ten lo-fi studios, occupied by new-wave talent such as Fiona Beveridge, Nathan Anthony and Theo Cleary, and a flexible exhibition space. The adventurous, often avant-garde programme has included video works, illustration, sculpture and installation; a 2016 show by Edinburgh College of Art grad Iain Sommerville, 'Dumb Marotte', combined a series of rather lewd charcoal drawings with a marionette performance. Come here to see what's fuelling the grassroots scene. *188-190 Pleasance, www.thenumbershop.org*

18.30 Glenogle Swim Centre

A paean to the Victorian predilection for self-improvement, this is one of several late 19th-century and early 20th-century swimming pools still in operation across the city. Of those that are accessible to the public, council-run Glenogle Baths (as it's known round here) is the most central, sandwiched in-between the Georgian splendour of Saxe-Coburg Place and the quirky listed 'colony' houses off Glenogle Road that were built as a philanthropic endeavour. Go for a well-deserved swim to admire the architecture from the water as you exercise. In the lead-up to the site's 2010 refurbishment, local campaigners persuaded the powers-that-be to keep the glass ceiling, gallery and poolside cubicles that give the place so much atmosphere. *Glenogle Road, T 343 6376, www.edinburghleisure.co.uk*

20.30 Edinburgh Food Studio

Chefs Ben Reade and Sashana Souza Zanella (see p062) met while they were studying at the University of Gastronomic Sciences in Piedmont, and decamped to Edinburgh to launch the Food Studio in 2015. The restaurant is only open three nights a week (Thursday to Saturday) and offers a sublime seven-course tasting menu, built around ingredients sourced on the day; past dishes include a lobster bisque with turbot dumplings, and pickled mackerel on potato mousse. A paired wine list focuses on natural producers. The vibe is that of a supper club, and diners gather either around two communal teak tables, or perch at an island bench. The botanical drawings, hung on dark-green panelling, are by Sulamith Wildgoose. Book ahead.
158 Dalkeith Road, T 258 0758, www.edinburghfoodstudio.com

URBAN LIFE
CAFÉS, RESTAURANTS, BARS AND NIGHTCLUBS

Edinburgh's culinary scene has been gaining a reputation as one of the best in the UK. Four of its chefs – Tom Kitchin (see p047), Martin Wishart at his eponymous Leith restaurant (see p058), Paul Kitching at 21212 (3 Royal Terrace, T 523 1030) and Jeff Bland at The Balmoral's Number One (1 Princes Street, T 557 6727) run Michelin-starred establishments. Joining these headline acts is a substantial supporting cast. At Aizle (107-109 St Leonard's Street, T 662 9349), Stuart Ralston and Krystal Goff offer a set five-course menu based on a monthly 'harvest', promoting a near-evangelical sense of seasonality, while the Edinburgh Food Studio (see p039) is part gourmand workshop, part fine-dining hotspot.

Then there's the spin-offs. Wishart's French-inspired brasserie The Honours (see p058) is often fully booked, as is Tom Kitchin and Dominic Jack's Stockbridge gastropub The Scran & Scallie (1 Comely Bank Road, T 332 6281). Over the road, Rollo (108 Raeburn Place, T 332 1232) is a chic tapas and wine bar, while Andrew and Lisa Radford's Timberyard (see p048) is still making waves.

Most pubs are welcoming, but some can be sniffy to non-locals. Bars are less risky: Bramble (see p042) is still the drinking den du jour, the Whiski Rooms (4-7 North Bank Street, T 225 7224) offers more than 300 malts, or try The Voodoo Rooms (19a West Register Street, T 556 7060) for live music and glam surroundings.
For full addresses, see Resources.

Cafe St Honoré

This dimly lit brasserie – with crisp white tablecloths, chequerboard floors and walls lined with mirrors – would not be out of place on the Left Bank. Chef Neil Forbes prepares classic French dishes, but his produce is anchored in Scotland – Forbes is fastidious about sourcing ingredients from local suppliers and foragers; and the restaurant also practises nose-to-tail butchery. The seasonal à la carte menu changes daily, and includes dishes like confit duck using poultry sourced from Gartmorn Farm in Alloa and North Sea coley brandade with *sauce vierge* (olive oil, lemon juice, chopped tomato and basil). Don't skip dessert, which might be a pert wild-mint crème brûlée. The wine list is similarly devoted to organic producers.
34 North West Thistle Street Lane,
T 226 2211, www.cafesthonore.com

The Lucky Liquor Co

Mike Aikman and Jason Scott, the pair behind late-night haunts Bramble (T 226 6343) and The Last Word (T 225 9009), opened The Lucky Liquor Co in 2013. It has the feel of a polished bistro, with an oak-topped bar at the rear clad in white subway tiles. Choose from 13 seasonal cocktails, which often mix house-made liqueurs and unusual ingredients.
39a Queen Street, T 226 3976

Restaurant Mark Greenaway

One of 2013's most anticipated openings was the relocation of Mark Greenaway's progressive British restaurant to the New Town from Picardy Place. The dining room, in a renovated Georgian townhouse with interiors designed by Four-by-Two, melds eye-catching clusters of Victorian brass chandeliers with teal walls and oversized mirrors overlaid with maps of Edinburgh. This is an excellent spot to satiate a sweet tooth – try the chocolate tart served with custard jelly, crème fraiche parfait, salted caramel and kumquat purée – though the modern, inventive starters and mains are of equally high quality. The building was once a bank and the extensive wine cellar, tended to by sommelier Jack Dickinson, is housed below inside the old vaults.
69 North Castle Street, T 226 1155, www.markgreenaway.com

The Shore Bar & Restaurant

One of the country's first gastropubs, The Shore opened its doors more than 30 years ago and has matured into a much-loved fixture on Leith's waterfront, its lively bar and cosy dining room – fitted wth darkwood panelling, large mirrors and an open fireplace – unchanged for years. Now owned by a local restaurant group, the focus is on seafood, such as smoked haddock and prawn risotto, as well as the pub classics, including lamb rump served with mint mash, ratatouille and port jus and, for dessert, a moreish treacle tart. Full menus are available from noon until 10pm seven days a week, and an unhurried, easygoing atmosphere persists. Befitting The Shore's casual appeal, there are plenty of wines available by the glass.
3 The Shore, T 553 5080,
www.fishersrestaurants.co.uk

Lowdown Coffee

This is a small, polished café, located in the bright basement of a Georgian terrace. The design – by local firm LLUC alongside owner Paul Anderson – is Scandinavian in feel, and features a sleek Corian, marble and oak serving counter and simple strip lighting; the minimal furniture is a mix of Alias and Källemo, while a spattering of potted plants add warmth. The beans are sourced from a rotating list of speciality suppliers, including Sweden's Koppi, Bath's Colonna, and April Coffee Roasters from Copenhagen. The team is just as exacting about tea, supplied by London's Postcard; try the sweet, toasty Yimu Oolong. Pick up delicious sandwiches, perhaps cornbread stuffed with roast vegetables, or baked goods, such as a rhubarb and sour cream loaf smeared with raspberry icing.
40 George Street, T 226 2132

The Kitchin

Owner and head chef Tom Kitchin draws a serious crowd to his Michelin-starred restaurant, located in a uniform row of eateries and bars on the waterfront in Leith. More than a decade on, and the hype is still justified. Glasgow-based firm Burns Design led a 2016 refurbishment, which introduced a private dining room and whisky snug, and a slew of textures: tweeds, naturally, as well as wallpaper by Timorous Beasties (see p018), sheepskins from the Isle of Skye, and stonework. The cuisine, served up on earthy tableware by Clare Dawdry, focuses on Scottish produce prepared using French techniques. From the seasonal menu, dishes include boned and rolled pig's head with langoustine tail, and Orkney scallops baked in the shell.
78 Commercial Quay, T 555 1755,
www.thekitchin.com

Timberyard

You cannot (and should not) miss Andrew and Lisa Radford's 2012 venture, which announces itself with an industrial-scale bright-red doorway near the College of Art. Timberyard is divided into multiple areas, each giving a nod to the venue's previous incarnation (the clue is in the name). The various spaces include the Shed (opposite), a brick outhouse for private dining that has a cosy wood-burner, and the Warehouse (above), where bare light bulbs hang from the high ceiling. The Radfords' son Ben directs the kitchen and produces artful dishes like sea trout with coastal herbs. Younger brother Jo helms the bar, serving up the sort of cocktails – sour beer mixed with fermented rhubarb and mead – that make you grateful for the bleak climes.
10 Lady Lawson Street, T 221 1222, www.timberyard.co

The Gardener's Cottage

A once dilapidated, listed 19th-century cottage now provides the setting for a taste of the country in the heart of the city. Edinburgh's seasonal and sustainable revolution continues to gain momentum here with chefs Edward Murray and Dale Mailley leading the way, their CVs loaded with stints in the capital's top restaurants, as well as their own temporary pop-up at Edinburgh Farmers' Market. The interiors were done on a tight budget yet the result is a pleasingly rustic spot with communal wooden tables, salvaged seating and china made by a local potter. The garden provides the herbs and vegetables, which feature on a neat daily menu that includes dishes such as roe deer with chanterelles, rowan berries and spelt. Closed Tuesdays.
1 Royal Terrace Gardens, T 558 1221, www.thegardenerscottage.co

Peter's Yard

Foster + Partners' redevelopment of the former Royal Infirmary (now known as Quartermile) may be rather uninspiring, but one of its redeeming features is this buzzy spot. The pale, clean-lined interiors by Norrgavel provide a refreshing change from the boho cafés that litter the city. Founded by Swedish master baker Peter Ljungquist, Peter's Yard entices customers through its glass doors thanks to a pile of rustic artisan breads on the counter. Inside, the café offers Scandinavian-style treats, a superb lunch menu, homemade conserves, mouth-watering desserts and cakes, gourmet chocolate and top-notch coffee. A second branch opened in 2012 in Stockbridge (T 332 2901). The signature sourdough pizzas here are a hit.
Quartermile, 27 Simpson Loan,
T 228 5876, www.petersyard.com

Earthy

The Earthy story began in 2008 in an old Southside printworks when a foodie, a farmer and a horticulturalist got together and hatched a plan to turn it into a 'food hub'. The resulting café and deli offers wholesome fare; dishes such as organic sweet potato, ginger and coconut milk soup are served alongside gourmet items and produce that come from around 200 Scottish growers and farmers, helping to bridge the time gap between the city's weekly markets. This homespun ethos also extends to the design, which features recycled timber salvaged from skips and seating made from wind-damaged trees by local craftsmen. The Earthy empire encompasses two other outlets: a shop in Portobello (T 344 7930) and a restaurant and food store in Canonmills (T 556 9696). *33-41 Ratcliffe Terrace, T 667 2967, www.earthy.co.uk*

Kanpai

The name means 'bottoms up' in Japanese, but this stylish sushi canteen is more of a place to sip sake than to down a few. The interior, devised by Leith-based agency Four-by-Two, is inspired by contemporary Tokyo sushi bars, with rhythmic slatted oak panels throughout and teal accents. The space is divided into three areas: the modern bar clad in rough-cut, solid timber blocks, where you can watch the Japanese-trained chefs at work; a private dining nook (opposite); and the minimal dining room itself (above), which has textured wallpaper cast with Japanese prints. As well as raw fish, the menu includes grilled dishes and teppanyaki, and there's a small but well-selected sake list: we recommend the full-bodied and dry Kasumi Tsuru.
8-10 Grindlay Street, T 228 1602,
www.kanpaisushi.co.uk

Chop House

Located in a former cork warehouse, Chop House is a buzzy restaurant with a menu, not surprisingly, almost entirely devoted to meat. The British beef, butchered on site, is dry-aged using Himalayan salts for up to 90 days before being cooked on the open-flame grill. Sharing is encouraged – the surf and turf, intended for two or more, consists of chateaubriand, a half lobster and dripping chips with béarnaise sauce. Or opt for a steak matched with a classic side like crispy gem lettuce dolloped with blue cheese. The diner-style interiors by Four-by-Two have an industrial bent – the bar is clad in steel, and there is a feature wall of pivoting glass panels – warmed up by the tangerine banquettes and marble elements. A smart sister spot (T 629 1551) was opened in Canongate in 2016.
102 Constitution Street, T 629 1919,
www.chophousesteak.co.uk

The Honours

For more than a decade and still counting, Martin Wishart's Leith restaurant (T 553 3557) has been enchanting foodies from Edinburgh and beyond. In 2011, the star chef's many acolytes gained a new place of worship when The Honours opened just off Queen Street. The brasserie, led by his right-hand man Paul Tamburrini, draws punchy flavours from Scottish produce, resulting in dishes such as ox cheeks with bordelaise sauce and apple purée, or globe artichoke risotto. The three-course lunch prix-fixe menu is fairly priced at £23. Long-standing collaborators Ian Smith Design conceived the smart interiors, and rather than emulate Wishart's subdued fine-diner, Smith got out his set square and protractor to create a confident geometric look.
58a North Castle Street, T 220 2513, www.thehonours.co.uk

Norn

Opened in 2016, Norn is a neighbourhood restaurant that has quickly earned itself a golden reputation for its inventive four- and seven-course tasting menus. The no-frills decor – beige walls, grey carpeting, lightwood chairs and industrial pendant lighting – is a natty foil for rotating dishes by chef Scott Smith, formerly of the Peat Inn. He sources ingredients locally, from speciality producers, and plates might include fermented turnip, smoked mussel, mugwort and cicely; or rabbit with peas, cockles and chickweed. The crusty bread (made with Orkney beremeal flour) and house whipped butter is worth showing up for alone. The wine list focuses on small-scale, natural and biodynamic producers. Closed Sundays and Mondays.
50-54 Henderson Street, T 629 2525, www.nornrestaurant.com

The Pompadour by Galvin

For many years, 'The Caley' was a faded fixture on Princes Street. That changed in 2012 when it became a Waldorf Astoria and got a £24m renovation. The Galvin brothers run the hotel's two restaurants, including The Pompadour, which serves French haute cuisine. The dining room features fabulously ornate plasterwork and restored hand-painted wallpaper.
Princes Street, T 222 8975

INSIDERS' GUIDE

BEN READE AND SASHANA SOUZA ZANELLA, CHEFS

Founders of Edinburgh Food Studio (see p039) Ben Reade, born and bred in the city, and Sashana Souza Zanella, who grew up in Montreal, live in the neighbourhood of Leith. 'It's gritty, eclectic and diverse,' says Souza Zanella. 'Bacon-roll shops sit next to high-end restaurants.' Indeed, they love that they can buy *lahmacun* (Turkish pizza) from Akdeniz Mediterranean Supermarket (82-90 Leith Walk, T 554 9248), antipasti from Italian delicatessen Gaia (32 Crighton Place, T 553 7333) and artisanal doughnuts from hip café/bakery Twelve Triangles (90 Brunswick Street, T 629 4664).

To relax, the pair might head to The Meadows. 'It feels young and alternative, and has a Central Park vibe.' Other favourite spots include the Old Town's cobbled lanes – 'they breathe history' – and the leafy paths around Dean Village. In Stockbridge, they make a beeline for both Artisan Roast (100a Raeburn Place) and Smith & Gertrude (26 Hamilton Place, T 629 6280), 'for great cheeses with amazing wines', before strolling nearby St Stephen Street: 'It has a bunch of wonderful, independent shops,' says Reade.

Further afield, they recommend a trip to the seaside town of North Berwick, half an hour away by train, where they suggest fuelling up at Steampunk Coffee (49a Kirk Ports, T 01620 893 030) and Bostock Bakery (42 High Street, T 01620 895 515) for a swim or brisk walk at Seacliff, and a poke around Tantallon Castle. *For full addresses, see Resources.*

ART AND DESIGN
GALLERIES, STUDIOS AND PUBLIC SPACES

The art scene here is a varied beast. There is, of course, a superb heavyweight collection stashed in the Scottish National Portrait Gallery (see po34), but there's also a group of nascent, artist-run spaces frothing with DIY invention: the Number Shop (see po36), Embassy (10b Broughton Street Lane) and Rhubaba (25 Arthur Street, T 629 8821) are three of the best. A more formal, yet no less exciting, arena is Talbot Rice Gallery's experimental TRG3 (see po71), which shines a spotlight on emerging talent. And small but smart commercial venues pack a punch too: Open Eye Gallery (34 Abercromby Place, T 557 1020) has exhibited the likes of Picasso, Joan Miró and David Hockney, and don't miss Ingleby (opposite).

The Edinburgh Art Festival was founded in 2004, and has since blossomed into a month-long bonanza of exhibitions and events staged right across the capital. Year-round, seek out works in the public realm: from Martin Creed's *No 1059* (see po70) to Antony Gormley's 2010 *6 Times*, consisting of six life-size figures, one of which is buried waist-deep in the pavement outside the Scottish National Gallery of Modern Art (75 Belford Road, T 624 6200).

There remains a strong affinity for the handmade here, and local design often exudes a minimal, Scandinavian aesthetic (see po94). Other makers channel classic Scottish craft and give it a fresh spin, such as hip weavers Squid Ink Co, available at Life Story (see po92). *For full addresses, see Resources.*

Ingleby Gallery

Founded in 1998 and undoubtedly one of Britain's most ambitious private galleries outside London, the Ingleby is one of the grandes dames of the Edinburgh scene yet manages to retain a freshness. It moved from this original townhouse setting to a larger site in 2008, setting up shop in a former nightclub behind Waverley Station, before returning in 2016. Owners Florence and Richard Ingleby helm a space suited to the tranquil appreciation of artists such as Peter Liversidge, Alison Watt, Howard Hodgkin, James Hugonin and the late Ian Hamilton Finlay. A 2016 show by Jonathan Owen (above) featured a series of forgotten 18th- and 19th-century marble statues that he brought back to life through recarving to create mutated, elegant new forms.
6 Carlton Terrace, T 556 4441,
www.inglebygallery.com

Stills

Scotland's Centre for Photography, Stills, was established in 1977, and puts on four exhibitions a year – often comprehensive shows of more established artists whose oeuvre has perhaps been rarely seen in the country before. The programme has ranged from a retrospective on Joseph McKenzie – who is considered the father of modern Scottish photography – to names like Peter Hujar and Chloe Dewe Mathews. In 2016, it hosted a hard-hitting presentation of the work of Jo Spence (above), which featured self-portraiture dating from the last years of her life, from 1968 to 1982. However, there's a focus on contemporary issues too; a series entitled 'Social Documents' explored themes such as migration, sexuality and globalisation. *23 Cockburn Street, T 622 6200, www.stills.org*

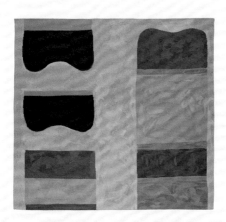

Dovecot Studios

This highly regarded but little-known gallery blends the city's past and present to great effect. The venue (overleaf) was previously the city's first public baths, in use from 1885 until 1995, when neglect forced its closure and it was left facing demolition. It was rescued by the world-class contemporary tapestry firm Dovecot Studios, which took up residence after a reinvention in 2009. It celebrated its centenary three years later, and weaving continues to be integral to the project. Today, Dovecot also collaborates with artists and curators to put on exhibitions and produce limited-edition works, such as this William Scott masterpiece entitled *Green and Blue Forms* (above). There is an on-site café run by local beanery Leo's.
10 Infirmary Street, T 550 3660, www.dovecotstudios.com

The Scotsman Steps

This deceptively simple public work was commissioned for the 2011 Edinburgh Festival by the Fruitmarket Gallery (see p028) as an extension of Martin Creed's exhibition 'Down Over Up', which explored the theme of progression, in height, size and tone: from totem-like stacks of chairs to a recording of a choir singing scales. For this piece, *No 1059*, the Turner Prize-winning artist remodelled the worn-out 1899 stairs that connect the Scotsman Hotel with Market Street, cladding them in 104 different colours of marble from around the globe. It's intended to highlight Edinburgh as an international city, while the classical material nods to historicism. It might be a stretch of the imagination too far, especially considering the Italian connotations, but Creed has described the work as 'a microcosm of the whole world'.

Talbot Rice Gallery

The University of Edinburgh's Talbot Rice encompasses three diverse spaces within Old College (see p080), each of them a real treat. Gallery 1 – a modern, minimal venue – hosts a programme of rotating exhibitions ranging from retrospectives like 'The Subject and Me', which explored the works of the postwar US painter Alice Neel, to shows by contemporary Scottish talent. Gallery 2 (above), in contrast, is a Georgian-era balconied hall designed by William Playfair as a natural history museum. The upper level displays bronzes and 17th-century Dutch paintings, part of a collection of 200,000 artefacts. Gallery 3, meanwhile, focuses its dynamic TRG3 programme on a challenging circular room. Closed Sundays and Mondays.
Old College, South Bridge, T 650 2210, www.ed.ac.uk

ARCHITOUR

A GUIDE TO EDINBURGH'S ICONIC BUILDINGS

The fact that Edinburgh is blessed with some of the finest historic buildings in the country makes it ideal for visitors, but it has been a huge burden on working architects based here. Until 20 years ago, there was essentially a moratorium on changing the landscape in the centre, which was in some danger of turning into a museum rather than the buzzing heart of a modern capital. However, the 1990s brought a need for office space and housing, and an easing of the draconian laws. It was acknowledged that the new could be successfully blended with the old, and the Scottish Storytelling Centre (see p081), Dovecot Studios' (see p067) repurposing of a derelict pool and the £150m spruce-up of Waverley Station – with a roof made of 28,000 glazed panels – finished in 2013 have been praised for stitching threads of modernity into the existing fabric.

Indeed, Edinburgh has grown so confident that it now boasts one of Britain's most innovative structures – in 2004, the Scottish Parliament (see p076) became a turning point for the city's built environment, although it is loved and loathed in equal measure. It helped pave the way for confident projects such as the £850m redevelopment of the St James mall that began in 2016 and will feature as its centrepiece a Jestico + Whiles-designed W hotel due in 2020. The facade will be wrapped in a spiralling bronze 'ribbon' that has already been likened by some locals to a Walnut Whip. *For full addresses, see Resources.*

National Museum of Scotland

Hot on the heels of the refurbishment of the Scottish National Portrait Gallery (see p034) came a large-scale overhaul of the Victorian section of the National Museum of Scotland (formerly the Royal Museum). The £47m undertaking, completed in 2011, resulted in the oldest part of the country's flagship museum (above) being restored to its glass-ceilinged glory by Glasgow architects Hoskins. Ten additional major galleries, devoted to science, design, art and, for the first time, fashion, opened in 2016. Due to the redevelopments, there's no longer an uncomfortable partnership between the rather careworn edifice and Benson & Forsyth's bold 1998 extension (overleaf), which is eye-catching in many ways, not least for its sentinel-like rotunda. *Chambers Street, T 0300 123 6789, www.nms.ac.uk*

Scottish Parliament

The late Catalan architect Enric Miralles' Parliament has caused no end of debate, and not just among MPs. Some regard the building as a disaster – energy-inefficient and poorly constructed (falling beams, a leaky roof, windows cracking and doors buckling), despite coming in three years late and 10 times over budget. Indeed, the issues surrounding its construction are still under scrutiny. Yet those who love it say it opened up the city's architectural arena for a freer approach, and praise a tour de force in local granite, concrete and decorative wood detailing that reflects the drama of the surrounding landscape. The experts agreed and it was awared the 2005 Stirling Prize, judge Piers Gough calling it a work of 'poetry, beauty, magnificence'. *Horse Wynd, T 348 5200, www.parliament.scot*

Royal Commonwealth Pool

Most locals tend to ignore this modernist triumph and head straight to the Olympic-size swimming pool inside. We'd advise you to linger and admire the aluminium-clad planes and deep overhangs that cleverly mask a sloping site, and the tall chimney that balances out the horizontal and nods to Arthur's Seat behind. It was designed by Robert Matthew, a protégé of the great Scottish architect Basil Spence, as a venue for the 1970 Commonwealth Games, and has proved popular with the public ever since. Known as the 'Commie', it reopened in 2012 after a £37m refurbishment that lasted nearly three years, and continues to function as a top-level training facility. A separate 25m pool with a new moveable floor hosted the diving at the 2014 Games. *21 Dalkeith Road, T 667 7211, www.edinburghleisure.co.uk*

Old College

It took the better part of a century to finish the home of Edinburgh University's School of Law. Work started in 1789 but architect Robert Adam died three years later and the funds soon ran out. The main structure was completed by William Playfair from 1819 to 1827, and then Sir Robert Rowand Anderson finally added the dome in 1879. A dramatic arch announces the entrance to Old College, and although its attractive courtyard was being employed as a car park until 2010, even that could not take away from the impact of Adam's landmark. In 2011, a grassed quadrangle that was proposed by Playfair in his original design, but which was never realised due to a lack of money, finally came to fruition with a plan and restoration by local firm Simpson & Brown. It is sympathetic to his vision.
South Bridge, T 650 8003

Scottish Storytelling Centre

In one of Britain's most protected urban zones, located halfway up the Royal Mile and attached to John Knox House, which dates to 1470, architects Malcolm Fraser have masterfully set the modern beside the ancient. The Scottish Storytelling Centre is a scheme that aims to revive a dying oral tradition, and the clarity of the unamplified spoken word was a key part of the brief. Take a peek inside to witness how the light, informal interior spaces of the contemporary intervention, which are lined with panels of Douglas fir, juxtapose almost effortlessly with the slice of history next door. This was formerly the site of the Netherbow Port, the principal gate into Edinburgh and part of its defences, and its 1621 bell now adorns the SSC's new tower.
43-45 High Street, T 556 9579,
www.tracscotland.org

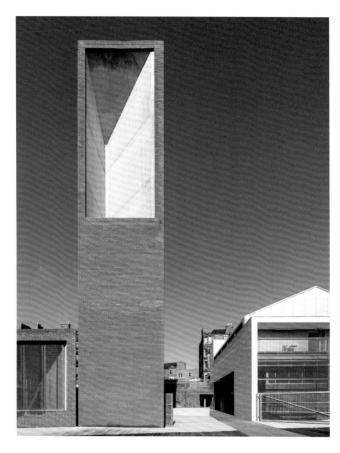

Edinburgh Sculpture Workshop

This was a rundown railway shed when the Sculpture Workshop colonised it in 1992. Two decades later, it was transformed by Sutherland Hussey Harris, who carved out a series of flexible spaces, as well as 30 artist studios straddling the embankment of a disused train track. Added in 2014, the Creative Laboratories is a low-slung new build with a cloistered courtyard, lined in panels of steel grating, that exhibits artworks and enables visitors to observe foundry projects in action, such as bronze casting. The complex's calling card is its 22.5m brick-clad tower (above). Influenced by a traditional Italian campanile, it emits a soft glow at night, ambiently illuminated from a large, angled aperture at its apex. On-site Milk café (T 551 5775) is open daily.
21 Hawthornvale, T 551 4490,
www.edinburghsculpture.org

Chapel of St Albert the Great

Simpson & Brown's minimal and graceful university chapel was consecrated in 2012. It is located in the garden of a Georgian townhouse (overleaf), and the materials at play reference its tranquil, leafy setting. Four tree-like Corten columns support an extensive series of arcing oak slats, which sweep, wave-like, over the altar and pews, and the roof is clad with flowering sedum, minimising its impact when viewed from above. A masonry wall, constructed from clay blocks faced with sandstone, feels both rich with historical allusion but still modern; its deep, angled windows allow in gentle natural light. So too does the glazed west wall, providing views of the changing seasons that play an important part in the worship calendar. It is open from 8am to 6pm. Access is via Middle Meadow Walk. *George Square*

Scottish Widows Building

A series of interlocking hexagonal volumes form the uncompromsing, eerie Scottish Widows HQ, which was unveiled in 1976 next to Holyrood Park. It seems somewhat at odds with its famously cheesy TV ads, but perhaps as brooding and mysterious as the woman in the cape. Predominantly constructed from reinforced concrete, it was designed by Sir Basil Spence, Glover & Ferguson to emulate the basalt strata of nearby Salisbury Crags. Its exterior is clad with brown-tinted solar glass, framed by bronze mullions, and York stone forms the lower walls. The various elevations, from one to four storeys high, are supported by columns that emerge from reflecting ponds (above). The sci-fi-like geometric blueprint is best appreciated from above; head up to Arthur's Seat for the best view.
15 Dalkeith Road

Royal Botanic Garden

Founded in the 1600s, the Royal Botanic Garden now extends over 28 hectares of exquisitely landscaped grounds just north of the town centre. An imaginative events programme keeps the public, as well as horticulture buffs, returning, more so than ever since the John Hope Gateway (above) opened in 2009. Named after the Garden's keeper from 1761 to 1786, it's a low-carbon build by architects Edward Cullinan that highlights environmental sustainability, from a wind turbine on the sedum roof to rainwater harvesting, a biomass-fuelled boiler and photovoltaic panels. There are slate walls and swathes of Scottish timber, in everything from the helical staircase to furniture; tabletops have been fashioned from trees previously felled on the site. *Arboretum Place, T 248 2909, www.rbge.org.uk*

SHOPS

THE BEST RETAIL THERAPY AND WHAT TO BUY

Princes Street and George Street vie for the title of Edinburgh's main shopping drag. Between the two stands Jenners (48 Princes Street, T 225 2442), Scotland's stateliest department store. Harvey Nichols (30-34 St Andrew Square, T 524 8388) is not far away, as is womenswear emporium Epitome (35 Dundas Street, T 556 5554); look out for the chic local cashmere label Cameron Taylor.

For specialist boutiques, steep and winding Victoria Street has several gems, including IJ Mellis Cheesemonger (No 30a, T 226 6215) and tailor Walker Slater (No 20, T 220 9750), which stocks its own line of smart tweed jackets and suits. You'll find covetable furniture and homewares at Moleta Munro (43-46 London Street, T 557 4800) and Catalog Ltd (2-4 St Stephen Place, T 225 2888), and visit Elk & Wolf (Arch 10, 19 East Market Street) for Scottish craft, like Emma McDowall's textured, coloured concrete vessels. A homegrown menswear scene is blossoming too. Check out The Brotique (opposite), Dick's (see p090) and Kestin Hare (see p093).

If you are on the hunt for edible treats, the Saturday farmers' market (9am to 2pm) on Castle Terrace is a must, as is a trip to German baker Falko Konditormeister (185 Bruntsfield Place, T 656 0763). Another essential is Italian deli Valvona & Crolla (19 Elm Row, T 556 6066), which also owns VinCaffè (11 Multrees Walk, T 557 0088), ideally located for a post-shopping coffee stop.

For full addresses, see Resources.

The Brotique

Gents' grooming has become big business in the capital, and there is now a slew of hip barbers to choose from, including Ruffians (see p026) and Rag & Bone (T 556 8200). The Brotique was established by Richard Murphy in 2014, and offers a bounty of oils, pomades and balms (the largest selection in the world, they say), including product from The Bearded Bastard, based in Austin, and Scots Hudson & Armitage, whose range uses natural ingredients and has aromas of cedar, tobacco and bergamot. There's also a collection of swank lifestyle items, from Ballanby's tweed dog collars to Jarre's AeroBull speakers, any of which you can choose – along with a badger-hair shaving brush, of course – to fill a bespoke hamper (cotton-lined with leather handles). *39 Queen Street, T 629 1303, www.thebrotique.co.uk*

Dick's

Former journalist Andrew Dick and his
wife, photographer Uli Schade, opened
Dick's in 2012, following a fruitless search
for an up-to-date Shetland jumper. You
you can now buy one here – look out for
Jamieson's wool crew necks. The shop is
brimming with practical, stylish garments,
from colourblocked sweaters, knitted in
Italy, by Andersen-Andersen and heavy-
duty Crescent Down Works parkas, as well
as homewares, like handwoven copper
baskets by Korbo. The store has a homey
feel, which might be due to Dick being
'fifth-generation Stockbridge'; his great-
grandfather had a tailor's shop on South
East Circus Place, just near here. The duo
designed the interior themselves, and it
melds custom furniture, made by a local
carpenter, with elegant Vitsoe shelving.
3 North West Circus Place, T 226 6220,
www.dicks-edinburgh.co.uk

Life Story

This concept store, launched in 2012, was originally the brainchild of husband-and-wife team Fee and Adam Storey, and it introduced a fresh retail experience to the capital. Susan Doherty took the reins in 2014, and expanded the simple honey-hued space, adding minimal pegboard displays and a small area at the rear for coffee and locally sourced baked goods; large windows offer garden views. The covetable range of furniture, homewares, accessories and lifestyle items is sourced from around the globe, including jewellery by London-based Wolf & Moon and washi tape from Japan, although Doherty puts an emphasis on Scandinavian designers: Hay stationery, Ferm Living textiles and sleek Hübsch ceramics are all sold here. *53 London Street, T 629 9699, www.lifestoryshop.com*

Kestin Hare

Established in 2014, Kestin Hare produces classic, unadorned casualwear for men in simple colours — usually greens, navy and neutrals. This flagship opened in 2015 (one of two stores in Scotland, alongside two London branches) and features clean, functional interiors, which include marble details, boxy flakeboard display units and wall-mounted copper grid sheets, used to display wares. Many of Hare's garments are produced in the UK, and made from speciality fabrications, like a traditional boiled-wool overcoat, which is updated with neoprene bonding, raw edges and powder-coated buttons; and wide-leg trousers cut from Japanese cotton. We would suggest you stock up on merino socks and Inverallan hand-knitted hats. *46 St Stephen Street, T 220 5859, www.kestinhare.com*

Natalie Wood

From her Albion Road studio in the north-eastern suburbs, designer Natalie Wood creates minimal ceramic works in muted pastel colours. She uses Parian clay, which is self-glazing and produces a matt texture, further enhanced by hand-polishing after firing. The 2015 'Detsu' line consists of a milky pink carafe (above), £30, cup and low pourer. Wood combines craft techniques with modern technologies; the simple, functional forms are inspired by basic structures used in 3D rendering software, for example. Other projects have included a bespoke range of colour-blocked, gently rimmed dinner plates that was produced for Moonfish Cafe, a stylish bistro based in Aberdeen. A selection of Wood's pieces is available to purchase at Life Story (see p092) or visit the studio by appointment. *www.nataliejwood.com*

Anta

For a tartan keepsake, skip the touristy shops flogging cheap tat on the Royal Mile and hit Anta, for everything from porridge bowls to woollen rugs, carpet bags and capsule clothing collections. Here, in the airy flagship store, instead of the bright red, yellow and blue of Royal Stewart, you will discover only stylish, Farrow & Ball-friendly tones: Highland heather mauve, Glencoe skies grey, and clootie dumpling taupe. Owners Annie and Lachlan Stewart are champions of artisan traditions, and much of their stock is made in Scotland, including the tweed woven in the Borders from yarn sourced from the Western Isles, and the chic oak furniture. If you are able, visit the Highland branch (T 01862 832 477) in Fearn, where many items are made. *119 George Street, T 225 9096, www.anta.co.uk*

ESCAPES

WHERE TO GO IF YOU WANT TO LEAVE TOWN

Edinburgh's modest size means that getting out is quick and easy. A short taxi ride can transport you to dramatic landscapes, while further afield, by car or train, are breathtaking surroundings and myriad outdoor activities, especially around Peebles to the south. Musselburgh is a quaint seaside fishing town that is convenient for a day trip. Less contaminated by amusement arcades and chip shops than its larger neighbour Portobello, it is home to one of the best gelaterias in Europe, S Luca (32-38 High Street, T 665 2237), open for business since 1908 and worth the 10km journey alone.

Self-catering properties are an ideal way to explore Scotland's hills, beaches and lochs. Desirable options abound. In the far north-west are contemporary Hill Cottage and Shore Cottage (bookable via www.croft103.com) and, further south, the eco-friendly Faire Chaolais (see p100). The Isle of Skye has a fine selection too. Timber House (www.timberhouse-skye.co.uk) and 15 Fiskavaig (Fiskavaig, T 07891 199 569) – both modern, airy retreats – are among its many hideaways, while The Three Chimneys restaurant and rooms (Colbost, T 01470 511 258) is a major part of the island's appeal. Or hop to the Highlands. Killiehuntly estate (By Kingussie, Highland, T 01540 661 619) encompasses a refurbished 1603 farmhouse with stylish interiors that mix Danish design and local craft, and just about all the produce used in the kitchen is grown on site.

For full addresses, see Resources.

Jupiter Artland, Wilkieston

Open from mid-May until mid-September, this art gallery and sculpture park, half an hour from Edinburgh by car, launched in 2009. Commissioning many of the major names in contemporary art to make work in situ in one reasonably compact space, co-owner Nicky Wilson has proved what can be done with a touch of vision – and some private investment. Fans of Charles Jencks' *Landform* at the Scottish National Gallery of Modern Art (see p064) can here admire his dramatic installation *Cells of Life* (overleaf), a series of vast, swirling earthwork knolls. It forms a mighty full-stop to a tour of large-scale pieces by Andy Goldsworthy, Antony Gormley, Cornelia Parker and others, which have included Jim Lambie (*ZOBOP (Fluorescent)*; above). *Bonnington House Steadings, T 01506 889 900, www.jupiterartland.org*

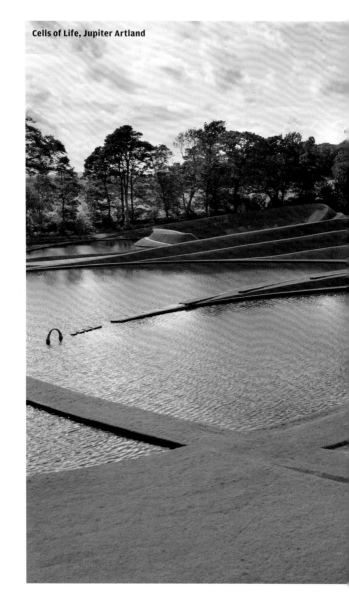

Faire Chaolais, Morar

This modern retreat – swathed in white paint and glossy concrete floors – is the work of Edinburgh architects Dualchas, who designed a larch-clad, gable-roofed structure. It cuts into an existing slope at its rear, cantilevering into the landscape, rather like a telescope. Indeed, the scenery is worth zooming in on; floor-to-ceiling glazing in the airy living space – simply furnished with plump leather sofas and a wood-fired stove – provides views to the small isles and the tidal Morar river. There is also a sleek kitchen illuminated by skylights (above), and three bedrooms on the ground floor. A pleasant three-hour drive from Edinburgh, it's an ideal spot to hang your hat for a few days and explore the surrounding Silver Sands beaches. *Morar by Mallaig, T 0131 441 7679, www.fairechaolais.co.uk*

The Falkirk Wheel

This engineering solution connecting the Forth and Clyde Canal with the Union Canal has not only restored navigability across Scotland, but the *Return of the Jedi*-like structure has also become an offbeat tourist draw. Opened in 2002, the world's first rotating boat lift replaces a tedious system of 11 locks that were dismantled in 1933. Boats entering the upper gondola are lowered, along with the water they float in, to the basin below (right). At the same time, an equal weight is raised in the opposing gondola. Don't get it? Take a trip yourself. Sailing from Edinburgh, you will pass through the Rough Castle Tunnel, under the historic Antonine Wall, to reach the Wheel, which elegantly cradles you 35m down to continue the journey to Glasgow. It is remarkably efficient – one turn uses the same energy as boiling eight kettles.
Lime Road, Tamfourhill, T 08700 500 208, www.scottishcanals.co.uk/falkirk-wheel

NOTES

SKETCHES AND MEMOS

RESOURCES

CITY GUIDE DIRECTORY

A

Aizle 040
107-109 St Leonard's Street
T 662 9349
www.aizle.co.uk

Akdeniz Mediterranean Supermarket 062
82-90 Leith Walk
T 554 9248

Anta 095
119 George Street
T 225 9096
Fearn
Tain
Ross-shire
T 01862 832 477
www.anta.co.uk

Artisan Roast 062
100a Raeburn Place
www.artisanroast.co.uk

B

Bostock Bakery 062
42 High Street
North Berwick
T 01620 895 515

Bramble 040
16a Queen Street
T 226 6343
www.bramblebar.co.uk

The Brotique 089
39 Queen Street
T 629 1303
www.thebrotique.co.uk

C

Cafe St Honoré 041
34 North West Thistle Street Lane
T 226 2211
www.cafesthonore.com

Cairngorm Coffee 025
1 Melville Place
T 629 1420
www.cairngormcoffee.com

Catalog Ltd 088
2-4 St Stephen Place
T 225 2888
www.cataloginteriors.com

Chapel of St Albert the Great 083
George Square

Chop House 056
102 Constitution Street
T 629 1919
Arch 15
East Market Street
T 629 1551
www.chophousesteak.co.uk

Collective 032
City Observatory and City Dome
38 Calton Hill
T 556 1264
www.collectivegallery.net

D

Dick's 090
3 North West Circus Place
T 226 6220
www.dicks-edinburgh.co.uk

The Dogs 030
110 Hanover Street
T 220 1208
www.thedogsonline.co.uk

HOTELS
ADDRESSES AND ROOM RATES

The Balmoral 016
Room rates:
double, from £235
1 Princes Street
T 556 2414
www.thebalmoralhotel.com

The Caledonian 060
Room rates:
double, from £210
Princes Street
T 222 8888
www.waldorfastoriaedinburgh.com

15 Fiscavaig 096
Room rates:
house, from £575 per week
Fiscavaig
Isle of Skye
T 07891 199 569
www.15fiscavaig.co.uk

Faire Chaolais 101
Room rates:
house, from £650 per week
Morar by Mallaig
T 0131 441 7679
www.fairechaolais.co.uk

G&V Royal Mile 018
Room rates:
double, from £180;
Garden Paradise Suite, from £650
1 George IV Bridge
T 220 6666
www.quorvuscollection.com

The Glasshouse 016
Room rates:
double, from £140
2 Greenside Place
T 525 8200
www.theglasshousehotel.co.uk

Hill Cottage 096
Room rates:
house, from £1,675 per week
Laid
Loch Eriboll
Sutherland
T 01971 511 202
www.croft103.com

The Howard 016
Room rates:
double, from £350
34 Great King Street
T 557 3500
www.thehoward.com

Killiehuntly 096
Room rates:
double, from £250;
farmhouse, £2,000 per night
(two-night minimum stay)
By Kingussie
Highland
T 01540 661 619
www.killiehuntly.scot

Motel One 016
Room rates:
double, from £70
18-21 Market Street
T 220 0730
10-15 Princes Street
T 550 9220
www.motel-one.com

94DR 020
Room rates:
double, from £120;
The Bowmore, from £150
94 Dalkeith Road
T 662 9265
www.94dr.com

Nira Caledonia 016
 Room rates:
 double, from £150
 6-10 Gloucester Place
 T 225 2720
 www.niracaledonia.com

The Pavilion at Lamb's House 021
 Room rates:
 house, from £300 per night
 (three-night minimum stay)
 11 Waters' Close
 T 467 7777
 www.lambspavilion.com

Prestonfield 022
 Room rates:
 double, from £325;
 Benjamin Franklin Suite, from £425
 Priestfield Road
 T 225 7800
 www.prestonfield.com

Principal 016
 Room rates:
 double, from £160
 19-21 George Street
 T 225 1251
 www.phcompany.com

Shore Cottage 096
 Room rates:
 house, from £1,650 per week
 Laid
 Loch Eriboll
 Sutherland
 T 01971 511 202
 www.croft103.com

The Three Chimneys 096
 Room rates:
 double, from £350
 Colbost
 Dunvegan
 Isle of Skye
 T 01470 511 258
 www.threechimneys.co.uk

Tigerlily 019
 Room rates:
 double, from £240;
 Black Room, from £450;
 Georgian Suite, from £550
 125 George Street
 T 225 5005
 www.tigerlilyedinburgh.co.uk

Timber House 096
 Room rates:
 house, from £650 per week
 6 Skinidin
 Isle of Skye
 T 557 4800
 www.timberhouse-skye.co.uk

The Witchery 017
 Room rates:
 double, from £325;
 Old Rectory Suite, from £325;
 Heriot Suite, from £325
 Castlehill
 The Royal Mile
 T 225 5613
 www.thewitchery.com

WALLPAPER* CITY GUIDES

Executive Editor
Jeremy Case

Author
Lucy Gillmore

Deputy Editor
Belle Place

Photography Editor
Rebecca Moldenhauer

Junior Art Editor
Jade R Arroyo

Editorial Assistants
Catalina L Imizcoz
Elena Gusperti

Contributors
Alex Bagner
Rhiannon Batten

Interns
Josie Finlay
Phoebe Lindsley
Margaux Sarginson
Alex Williams

Production Controller
Nick Seston

**Marketing & Bespoke
Projects Manager**
Nabil Butt

Wallpaper*® is a
registered trademark
of Time Inc (UK)

First published 2008
Fourth edition 2017

© Phaidon Press Limited

All prices and venue
information are correct
at time of going to press,
but are subject to change.

Original Design
Loran Stosskopf
Map Illustrator
Russell Bell

Contacts
wcg@phaidon.com
@wallpaperguides

More City Guides
www.phaidon.com/travel

Phaidon Press Limited
Regent's Wharf
All Saints Street
London N1 9PA

Phaidon Press Inc
65 Bleecker Street
New York, NY 10012

Phaidon® is a registered
trademark of Phaidon
Press Limited

www.phaidon.com

A CIP Catalogue record for
this book is available from
the British Library.

Printed in China

ISBN 978 0 7148 7374 9

PHOTOGRAPHERS

**Canestraro &
Di Pasquale**
Edinburgh Castle,
pp010-011
Fourth Rail Bridge,
pp014-015
The Witchery, p017
94DR, p020
Prestonfield, pp022-023
Cairngorm Coffee, p025
Ruffians, p026
Fruitmarket Gallery,
pp028-029
Scottish National Portrait
Gallery, p034, p035
Number Shop, pp036-037
Edinburgh Food Studio,
p039
Cafe St Honoré, p041
The Lucky Liquor Co,
pp042-043
Restaurant Mark
Greenaway, p044
Lowdown Coffee, p046
The Kitchin, p047
Timberyard, p048, p049
The Gardener's Cottage,
p050
Earthy, pp052-053
Kanpai, p054, p055
Chop House, pp056-057
Norn, p059
The Pompadour by Galvin,
pp060-061

Ben Reade and Sashana
Souza Zanella, p063
Stills, p066
Talbot Rice Gallery, p071
Chapel of St Albert the
Great, p083, pp084-085
Scottish Widows Building,
p086
The Brotique, p089
Dick's, pp090-091
Life Story, p092
Kevin Hare, p093
Anta, p095

Artur
Scottish Parliament, p077

Benjamin Blossom
McEwan Hall, p012
National Monument, p013
The Shore Bar &
Restaurant, p045
Peter's Yard, p051
National Museum of
Scotland, p073, pp074-075
Royal Commonwealth
Pool, pp078-079
Old College, p080
Scottish Storytelling
Centre, p081

Matt Clayton
Glenogle Swim Centre,
p038
Dovecot Studios,
pp068-069

Gautier Deblonde
The Scotsman Steps, p070

**Jerry Driendl/
Getty Images**
Edinburgh city view,
inside front cover

Getty
Scottish Parliament, p076

Matthew Laver
John Hope Gateway, p087

Andrew Lee
Faire Chaolais, p100, p101

David McKenna
Edinburgh Sculpture
Workshop, p082

John McKenzie
Ingleby Gallery, p065

Keith Hunter
Jupiter Artland, p097

Rebecca Moldenhauer
Natalie Wood, p094

Jackson Pollok-Morris
Jupiter Artland,
pp098-099

EDINBURGH
A COLOUR-CODED GUIDE TO THE HOT 'HOODS

LEITH
Once a gritty port in north-east Edinburgh, the waterfront is now sought-after real estate

SOUTHSIDE/NEWINGTON
This sprawling borough is characterised by green spaces, academic buildings and theatres

NEW TOWN
A feast of Georgian architecture, James Craig's urban idyll is city planning at its finest

OLD TOWN
Sidestep the tourist traps to marvel at the medieval splendour of this World Heritage site

WEST END/TOLLCROSS/BRUNTSFIELD
Gentrifying fast, these zones are now home to the middle classes, chichi stores and delis

CANONGATE
Numerous historic and modern landmarks are packed into this small corner of the city

For a full description of each neighbourhood, see the Introduction.
Featured venues are colour-coded, according to the district in which they are located.